The
O
in the
Air

Colosseum Books

James Matthew Wilson, series editor

The O in the Air

Poems by
Maryann Corbett

Franciscan University Press

Franciscan University Press
1235 University Boulevard
Steubenville, OH 43952
740-283-3771

Distributed by:
The Catholic University of America Press
c/o HFS
P.O. Box 50370
Baltimore, MD 21211
800-537-5487

Library of Congress Cataloging-in-Publication Data
Names: Corbett, Maryann, author.
Title: The O in the air : poems / by Maryann Corbett.
Description: Steubenville, OH : Franciscan University Press, [2023] |
    Summary: "This collection of poems by Maryann Corbett explores the
    heavenly aspects of the ordinary world: its beauty, pain, squalor, and
    glory. Both visionary and earthy, these pieces clash as the poet
    examines the world around her and finds connections to the divine.
    Deeply Catholic, Corbett is both animated and troubled by her faith,
    penning these poems to share with readers the never-ending quest to find
    answers to the mystery of our origins and our being"— Provided by
    publisher.
Identifiers: LCCN 2023009512 | ISBN 9781736656167 (paperback)
Subjects: LCGFT: Poetry.
Classification: LCC PS3603.O7323 O15 2023 | DDC 811/.6—dc23/eng/20230227
LC record available at https://lccn.loc.gov/2023009512
Text and Cover Design: Kachergis Book Design
Cover Image: Sherry O'Keefe
Printed in the United States of America.

Contents

❖ III

The O in the Air

Back Story

There is a category of northern European art in which a panoramic view, often a landscape, is the principal subject, while a classical or biblical scene appears as a distant detail.

The foregrounds are ablaze with the mundane—
a Renaissance reality, but real,
though magicked with the North's painterly light.
Take Breughel's. (Auden did, although we question,
these days, if it *was* Breughel's.) Or one might
ponder Teniers. Up front: the world and the flesh.
So solid you think of stepping into the canvas
to the plowed ground, or hefting the armor's weight.
Yet in the distance, a few brushstrokes of fable—
the boy with wings, the prisoner freed by the angel,
mere specks you have to sift for, with attention—
yank the scene by its ears and flip it over,

as if to ask, What strange spell are you under
that you go dazzled by life's pure distraction
and daylight's daze? Do not fall prey to the demon
who soothes you with the steadiness of fact.
Look here. The whole scene's leavened with this lightness.
Step back and stare at the mist beyond this frame,
these layers of ground earth and mineral spirit.
It's there, if you look past mere vision's weakness.
The question, always haunted by its answer:
What if the world you learned in flame and darkness
is apprehended only through these fancies?
What if the whole of it is heavenly?

I

Before

This is the one: the picture from before.
More beautiful than you have ever seen them,
they stand together in front of their first house,
in eight-by-ten matte silence, black and white.

More beautiful than you have ever seen them:
she—dark shirtwaist dress, open-toed shoes;
he—neatly mustached. His black-and-white
wingtips leap from the page: high-contrast joy.

Everything here is joyful. Open-toed shoes
place them postwar, these lovers, thoroughly lovely.
They've put off life for decades, starved for joy.
Now they pose with hydrangeas, in love with the world.

Like every couple in love, they are thoroughly lovely
so that you wonder, What happened? Could they not
have kept those lineless faces, in love with the world,
though open toes and wingtips would disappear?

You wonder, yet you know the answer. Not
some dark catastrophe: *You* were what happened.
You, so deeply dreamed, made smiles disappear.
Frowning child who lived in imagination,

you were the *kata strophe,* the turn that happened.
A problem from Greek drama, that parents' wanting
should bend the arc of a child's imagination
away (you think, watching your children go);

a problem out of tragedy, this wanting.
What happens when we clench our fists on dreams:
mistakes (you think, watching your children go).
Mark-missing. Hamartia. Feeling unwhole.

But here no fists seem clenched. With light-held dreams
they stand together in front of their first house
where no one rested long or felt as whole
as in this scene, this picture from before.

Sorrowful Mysteries

I.

Grinning jack-in-the-box,
it jolts from your mind at rest,
some bugbear out of childhood.

A word, a tone, a grimace
no grown-up meant you to see.

Through a glass of years, darkly,
it gathers shape, then fades.

There is no one alive to explain it.

II.

Late. Very late, and why was I awake
to hear the knock, the opening front door,
a pause, a muffled sob, and the name "Justine!"
urgently spoken, in my father's voice?
I stood. Opened my bedroom door a crack.
That name: someone they drank with once a year,
she and her husband. Old friends. What did it mean,
her strangled weeping, that sob-gasping noise?
Why were my parents bundling her indoors
to the spare bedroom? And once she was inside,
what were they whispering—clipped, tense—to each other?
I caught the word "police"—my mother's hoarse,
high whine. And then he saw me there, my father,
and ordered me, too sternly, back to bed.

III.

I'd helped address the Christmas cards
to the names kept in my mother's book.
Here, from a name I hadn't seen,
was a card set out for a second look

on the doily-covered dining table.
A note in cursive, hard to read—
not much an eight-year-old was able
to puzzle out of what it said,

the only hint my father's frown,
his gruff "*She's* got a hell of a nerve,
writing us here." He tossed it down.
They let the conversation swerve.

IV.

Her hands, lifted in horror to her mouth,
were hard to understand. Yes, it was dark;
yes, he was late. But here he was, so happy,
swaying a little as he pantomimed
the way it all went down, the storytelling
always his favorite role. How he had guided
the fraught negotiations to their yes,
how all the men in pinstriped suits had praised him,
how many times they'd drunk each other's health—
how many? had he counted the Manhattans?—
before they'd helped him get behind the wheel
to weave the hourlong way back home to her
and the children who were not supposed to see
her stand there, covering her mouth in fear.

V.

This is childhood's essence:
always to grope in the dark.

What the grip finds, it hoards
to worry in its fingers.
To tell, like rosary beads.

Ghazal for a Bottle of Shalimar, 1956

The clear amber scent in its bottle. Its glint from the top
   of the vanity:
cut-crystal flutes with a frosted-glass stopper, catching
   the sun, on her vanity.

The glamorous dreams of our mother, unspoken to
   curious children,
were sharp as the quarter-moon curve of that bottle
   enshrined on the vanity.

What were they guarding, what secrets? And how would
   a child understand them?
And what was I thinking, small magpie lured on by the
   glitter of vanity?

Wreckage of beauties: the spill. The wet, the gray film on
   the rosewood.
I was the firstborn, the first to drive thorns through the
   heart of her vanity.

Painfully, mothers forgive. (On the mountain with seven
   storeys,
how long will the granite of penitence weigh on the
   spine of *my* vanity?)

(And what do *my* children remember? What hauntings
   by anger and tears
does my memory hide from itself in the metal-bound
   chest of my vanity?)

Sixty years on, and the stain-mottled dresser now
   broods in my bedroom,
breathing regret, and my name, and the words of the
   Preacher: *Vanity!*

Overture

Be praised, Lord,   for propped-open windows.
In the muggy meanness   of mid-July,
they speak reassurance.

In the next yard,   high voices yammer—
small boys brandishing   brave new insults
from the old playbook,

while otherwhere   across the alley
the tantrum wail   of a wild toddler
repeats, *da capo*.

Will there be, this year,   young housemates warring,
screen doors that whomp,   wheels grinding gravel?
In this heat, wake us.

Send us street theater,   at three in the morning,
mad lovers battling   over jealousies, bills,
the whole grand opera.

Watch now in mercy   those others, mum
in the iced quiet   of their central air,
their curtained sorrows.

High

We were grounded for life: To be growing up
out in the suburbs, when they were new,
was to live life on a single storey:
rambler and ranch style, in homes
neatly bagged in cul-de-sacs;
at schools, too, low-slung and sprawling
over assorted boxy annexes;
at our stolid red-brick churches;
at shopping malls, then just beginning
to stretch their asphalt pseudopods
rectangularly over farms;
in every place children could go,
life was flat, earthbound,

so that a part of the rare delight
of visiting city relatives
was the rush of finally being somewhere,
anywhere, past the first floor.
Not until high school could we look
from windows into the crowns of trees;
not until college could we live
on third floors and look out on rooftops.
And what rooftops! Gables, gambrels,
mansards, slate and shakes, clay tile,
federal period chimney pots.
So when we came to own a house
and looked, oh bliss, from an upstairs porch
to the shingled roofs of our city neighbors,
we knew it: we'd come up in the world—

Son and daughter, reared in this house,
when you return, as you briefly do
in visits from your high-rise aeries,
will unaccustomed lines of sight
have stunned you into strange perspectives?
Yes, my darlings. Don't look down.

Magnification

Sand at 400x

Color comes as a shock.
Pink garnet, hematite, green epidote.
Agate, the jewels' blood.
      What's underfoot
is gemstone, not dumb rock,

and what we took for dun-
dusted utility—construction grade,
anonymous as mud—
      is scaled-down jade.
Like reliquary stone,

it venerates remains:
foraminifera in starch-stiff curls,
  puff-bodied, spiculed rays,
      whorled shells.
Silly to call them *grains*

as if a summer acre
busheled them, cut and dried, the season's yield.
These need the ocean's pace—
decades laid down like nacre,
      time pearled.

Drawn to this intimate view,
we're pressed to think in eons: glacial crush
that ground scree and moraine,
      and river rush
boiling the stone stew

down to a settled thing.
So brokenness, shivered from what it was,
    reduced again, again,
           till it seemed to us
    not worth our focusing,

    falls into focus, strong,
million-powered beneath the microscope
    while a girl with a paper cup
builds on the sand. What has borne up so long
    will bear her up.

Ghazal of Difficult Roses

All winter long I have these dreams of roses.
The six-month curse of winter bleeds to dreams of roses.

My mother loved them; thus my long obsession.
The barbed logic, the prickly enthymemes of roses.

The summer's chain-link fences heady with Peace:
Childhood was salmons, yellows, blush-and-creams of
     roses.

The statues in the War Memorial gardens
are without speech, but for the scarlet screams of roses.

Comfort me with old hues, old fragrances.
These strange new shades like bruises—they blaspheme the
     roses.

Who was the first to imagine prayers as blossoms?
Half-conscious minds meander through their streams of
     roses.

My confirmation saint was Rose of Lima,
who grasped the thorns of the most deep extremes of roses.

Late-Night Thoughts while Watching the History Channel

Is it by God's mercy
     that children are born not knowing
     the long reach of old pain?

That the five-year-old, led by the hand
     past the graffiti, cannot fathom
     his mother's tightening grip,

or why, when a box of nails
     clatters to the tile like gunfire,
     his father's face contorts?

So slow is the knitting of reasons,
     the small mind's patching of meaning from such ravel

as a cousin's offhand story,
     or a yellowed clipping whose old news
     flutters from a bottom drawer,

or some bloodless snippet of history
     dully intoned as you doze off, in the recliner—

so slow that only now, in my seventh decade,
     do I turn from these sepia stills,
     this baritone voiceover, chanting
     the pain of immigrant forebears,
     my thought impaled on a memory:

my twelve-year-old self, weeping
    on Sundays fifty years ago
    when my father drove us to Mass
    but stood outside, puffing his Chesterfields,

doing what his father had done,
    and his father's father before him,
    wordless to tell me why.

Knowledge

Scumbag. I'd like to punch him in the face.
Which makes no sense. He's dead, or he's so old
he's pitiable. So no: I *really* want
a time machine to 1937
to punch him then, the louse who deserted my mother
a dozen years before she met my father—
who waltzed away when the world was going to hell.
It's all laid out, the story she wouldn't tell me.
It's here, in the letter-sized accordion file,
the mess of records I'm charged with making sense of
(now mine, as child with power of attorney)
in ratty boxes on the bedroom floor.
Downstairs, the tinseled crumbs of the Christmas season
lie untidied. Our grown-up children bicker,
Tchaikovsky a glaze of sugar on the tensions.
Boxing me in: the oddments of her life.

Would it have made a difference if I'd known—
a little girl in a fifties Catholic school?
Would knowing have been better than wondering why
my mother, pious in her silk-flower hats
and spotless gloves, never received communion?
Better than guessing who he was, that man—
uniformed, dapper, his arm around her shoulders—
in the pictures shoved to the back of the bottom drawer
and found in the hours of childhood's summer boredom?
Better than fending off the curious questions
(*Isn't your mom a Catholic? Isn't your dad?*)
uttered in innocence in grade-school lunchrooms
between wrapped sandwiches and cartoned milk?

Better than fear when my father muttered *Bullshit,*
there at the pocked Formica kitchen table,
when I parroted the parts of the catechism
that covered the Church's marriage laws? Or better
than awkwardness a month before my wedding?
My whined insistence: general communion.
Her tight-lipped *No*; then my demand for reasons
and her pained face. Those shreds of information,
the dull fact of divorce, no more. Bare bones:
the dead past dead, its inconvenient skeleton
hanging behind the out-of-season woolens—

I have no answer. But here they are, these pages,
the heavy-paper forms of the Marriage Tribunal.
Annulment papers, filed in her old age
when the Church decided, finally, to be human,
decades too late to patch a childhood's bruises,
pointless except to let her take the host.
A name (that letter embroidered on old linens—).
His infidelities, detailed too shyly.
(I see her pacing a prewar flat in tears.)
Recitals of war, enlistment, army career
(and here my head fills in from textbook photos).
The postings far away, the letters rarer,
the money too, all finally disappearing.
More papers: kindly notes from the attorney
who handled the simple divorce she filed herself.

Then a new page: a kind of miracle play
of the mundane. A second chance: someone

who loved her. Nothing much to look at, no.
(I know this part; I have the earliest pictures,
in awful forties bathing suits. Rehoboth.
The joyful faces, oh, and the lumpy bodies.)
So bad a Catholic he didn't mind her past.
Here was a way to right her life again,
to write the rat, the scumbag, out of the story,
to be the leading lady, married and Catholic.
In the days when almost no one went to communion,
what would it matter, having to stay away?
This was a deal. Was it God who was saying, *Take it?*

She took it, and we lived its darker meanings:
The dancing away from even the simplest answers
(Where did you go to high school? Who did you like?)
Shushing my aunts and uncles if their gossip
careered too near the sheer drop of the facts.
Cutting them off mid-sentence and mid-gesture,
my mother disappearing around the bend
of a conversation's lurching hairpin turn.
The awkward years while the Church writhed in its changes
and the simple ruse of sitting still in the pew,
with everyone, was changed to an awkward shuffle
of choosing the back row or moving aside
as aisles of people streamed to the altar rail.

So now I know, or know how little I know.
I hold the pages, weighing my emotions:
Now there's a name to pin it on, a person.
I think of finding his nursing home, his grave.
I think of seizing his bony shoulders and shaking,
and shouting—*Bastard! Scumbag!*—at his face
as if it were he who'd bored a hole in my childhood.
Which makes no sense. The story is what it is.
It says he left; it keeps my mother's silence.
What pierces is her voice, her fierce insistence,
her sharp *I'm Catholic. Can't be anything else.*

I fold the papers up and pack them away.
Now they are mine. Mine is the only memory
she has. She has good care; I handle her business
and visit when I can, and talk of nothing,
but wince when she asks, *where is your father* (dead),
your sister (dead), and fresh pain clouds her face
at every new remembering. No use now
to ask what happened seventy years ago.

The last notes of the *Nutcracker* decay.
I plod downstairs. Just four of us, too few
for much of a celebration. Very quiet.
We're just not storytellers, my daughter sighs.
I murmur, *No.* The rest I leave unspoken.

Matinee

A dark universe, this one, its few stars
shoe-level pinpricks, red, as I pad in
amid torn candy wrappers and spilled popcorn.

This is the world in which I am The Chosen:

the world where I (despite my dorky hornrims,
epic gray frizz, old jeans that bag at the knee,
and inner baggage) rescue humankind
by seeing them as I saw them at fourteen:

The enemies, reptilian or mechanic,
long-fanged, or hissing, with great swathes of cape.
The crystalline hurricanes of CGI.
The motley and intrepid band of friends,
victorious, sailing toward a peach-tint sunset.

How then, reentering the gray-faced light
of middle age and ordinary time,
where only the late-winter drizzle glitters,
how will I recognize the hero's test?

Clutched in the monstrous tentacles of the day—
the screamed headline, the bank balance, the awful
mysteries of newfangled third-grade math—
alas, I cross distractedly at the light

and pass him without speaking, the great mage
disguised as a homeless beggar with a sign.

Rereading the *Aeneid*, Book IV

Sting of a memory, roused from its coils in the roots of the Latin:

raising my voice to my teacher, right there in the hallway. I lost it—
my grip on the weave of the grammar, the veiled indirectness of
    footnotes.
Red-faced, incensed at her hint that not all of the weeping was Dido's.
Calling Aeneas a jerk and a rat, almost shouting that duty,
piety, vows to the gods were all lies.

                   And her face. And her eyebrows
(bristly and white and just visible under the edge of a wimple)
knitting. Then both of us suddenly silent. The bell. And then moving
stone-faced toward chemistry class, while across on the opposite
    stairwell,
slouching, a certain young *perfidus* carefully stared at his loafers.

Fibs for a Construction Zone

*Pavement marking code: blue for water, red for
power, yellow for gas, green for sewer*

Eyes
down:
Sidewalks
gone dotty,
dashes in spray paint
Morse-coding streets kiddy-colored—

Can't
chalk
this up
to child's play.
It's the how-to where
all our digging at past troubles

lays
bare
wired-up
brokenness.
Old stinks we'd let lie.
Grown-ups' muddled entanglements—

Road,
work:
Tamp them
down again.
Slather gravel's gray
poultice over these ragged wounds.

Re-
draw
days in
hopscotch. Dot
them with tricycles
left on walks in summer twilight.

Lavoro all'uncinetto

Collection of Italian needlework pieces, circa 1920

Out of the depths (stuck bottom drawer, old chest)
I've dug from plastic-bagged indignity
a mound of lace meringue: fine white crochet,
mine now by force of law, and loss, and mess.
My mother's hoarding of her mother's handwork,
chastely intact, most of a century.

    Mysterious nonna, *visited*
    too rarely, poorly understood
    (our lost words locked each other out;
    our only common tongue was food)
    I never watched you, in bad light
    inventing beauty thread by thread.

What were they for? In the exuberant fifties,
my mother set them everywhere, such foam-spun
indulgences as social climbers prize.
O dresser scarves, O tablecloths, O doilies
spume-white against her dark mahogany!
Useless but for one virtue: looking *nice.*

    Scholarly monographs explain
    how whitework, hung from balconies
    in Naples on procession days,
    could air a daughter's worthiness
    for marriage. Streets of froth and fizz!
    (They make me queasy, facts like these.)

Pinned to the chubby arms and backs of sofas.
Small snowy rounds under the family portraits
and fragile porcelains on the tops of shelves
that held the books no one picked up to read.
The stuff of stiff-necked parlors, only used
for company. Too holy for ourselves.

> *What happens when the patterns change?*
> *When oceans rip a past away?*
> *Lacework that stood for luxury*
> *frayed to* lavoro. *Done for pay:*
> *chains into loops, loops into chains,*
> *managed between the labor pains.*

And holiness, subject to dust and ashes
(house dust, ash from my father's cigarettes,
impatient handling, children's grubby hands)
broke down. Then the tuition for two daughters
meant outside work. I watched her take the strain.
It was the sixties then. Of course I ran.

> *Bleach them all spotless. Starch and press.*
> *Plastic defends from pointless tears*
> *each noose around its nothingness.*
> *Hide them, untouched for fifty years.*
> *Never forget, though I forgot.*
> *Leave them to me: executress.*

What happens now? Who values patterned beauty?
Form on repeat, like rosaries or song?

It speaks constraint; perhaps it set her free
within its limits. Art strung out so long
is never simple, never a pure line.
All of its sad entanglements are mine.

> Nonna *I never really knew:*
> *my mother, last of your loved seven*
> *daughters and sons, is dead with you.*
> *From the white rose of Dante's heaven,*
> *mumble your clipped-Italian prayer*
> *over this frill of sound, of air.*

II

The Museum of American Opulence

We own too much. I'm thinking about a time
in the days when all we had in the world was each other,
a one-bedroom apartment, some wedding presents,
and a heated waterbed in a homemade frame.

Carless, we'd scrounge a dollar forty in change,
stand in the mean windchill of early December,
climb snowpile Alps to board, and take the 6
downtown, to the city's most *luxe* department store

to look. To gorge ourselves on staring at glitter,
at crystal chandeliers, at spotless chrome,
at the glassed-in cases where jewelry sat on velvet,

and then upstairs in housewares, the hundred patterns
of china and silver, the piles of towels and blankets,
the wild abundance long foretold by the prophets
and certain to be our own if we lived right.

And then we'd bus home, frozen and empty-handed,
red-faced, laughing, tumbling into the bed,
owning nothing, practicing pure desire.

Circadian Lament, Sung to a Wakeful Baby

Go back to sleep. You've made a slight mistake
switching your days and nights around this way.
The time will come for nights you spend awake,

for cough and colic, ear- and stomachache.
Though now you babble charmingly and play
the infant hours away (a light mistake),

there will be bitter medicines to take
some night. Take love: its wide-eyed thrills one day,
its clammy sweats the next. Take nights awake,

your soul in shreds, your bank account at stake,
your eyelids propped with stale café au lait.
Searching the stars for some obscure mistake

when futures cloud and omens turn opaque
and panic makes you pace the floors and pray—
There will be no escape from nights awake,

I warn you. And my wisdom doesn't make
one whit of difference. *Seize the night,* you say
in coo and babble. Ah, well. My mistake.
Instruct me in the joys of nights awake.

Ice Dam

The airiness of snow's accumulation
in powdery upheapings on the roof
swansdown-swaddled us through a muffled winter.
Only now, in the first whispers of March,
does the truth dribble down walls on the upstairs porch
with the full weight of what was always water,
fluid as mood and ponderous as grief,
an oozing, seeping, weepy accusation.
Now the recriminations; now we search
for scapegoats (insulation? fan? blocked gutter?)
but find there is no bargain-rate salvation.
This costs. Somebody has to risk his life.
The checkbook bleeds again. Abashed and bitter,
we beat our breasts for what was left undone.

Cold War

With all positions so hardened,
the ice thick on the sidewalks,
its rubble a scab over the ground,
one might be driven to foolish measures,
might take out the big electric demolition hammer
to bash at the rind on the front walkway
and end up with scarred concrete
and fifteen seconds of fame on the evening news
and the neighbors shaking their heads.
One might lose patience.

One might forget that at some point
the rubber boots will sink in the muddy ground,
that the handful of dirt thrown down in defiance
will break, as the ground itself breaks,
that at any moment the pink fists of the rhubarb
will raise their rebellion out of the thaw,
the spears of the peony pierce the soil
to aim their missiles toward a slow explosion
in million-petaled white clouds,
blood-red at the edges.

Schaar's Bluff: Upper Mississippi in April

Maples leafing out in their wild chartreuses
flash like neon over the river's margin,
garish next to paler and deeper greens of
    willow and jack pine.

Farther up the fields are prepared for seeding,
furrowed now, and distantly velvet-looking,
red-brown shading darkening into blackness
    over the hillcrest.

All against a blue that will not sit stable,
shifting with the wind-altered cloud and sun shifts,
dappling down to slate when the west goes coral,
    lavender, violet.

So much color: needless and utter blessing,
granting visions whether or not we sought them.
Once again I start with an empty canvas,
    sketching beginnings.

Differing Visions

Dear parent: Screening suggests that your child
may have red-green color blindness.
This should not be a cause for concern.

The couch she calls *maroon* her son calls *black*.
The hot pink espadrilles she always wears—
he says they're brown. Listen to her: she swears
now, and presses him. Her voice will crack:
Doesn't he see? The kid is five. She keeps
on drumming. *There, on the carpet, that green line—*
there, can you see it? Can't you? It grips the spine,
climbs to the brain, the chill tension that seeps
into her voice.
                    The evidence is cruel
but clear enough: he'll frame things differently,
in layered undertones she doesn't share.
The pigments that he'll grind of earth's blue jewel,
the gold archangels massed for him to see—
they're his. They'll riffle through her hands like air.

Waiting Up

Not home. Not home yet. Four a.m. Unknot me,
God whom I less than half believe my help.
Damp down the pounding underneath my scalp.
Unhook the gut-tight line of fear that's caught me
listening for cars, oh me of little faith.
They've seized their own lives, laughing, "Go to bed!"
And God, I hate her—hate the hag in my head
who mutters, praying through her gritted teeth,
make them come home, come home. God, shut her up.
Let me believe the thousand times they've come
home safe will make the door click one more time
and lock behind them. Free me from the trap
of thinking your ideas of *safe* and *home*
might not (my God!) be anything like mine.

Sung Passion

Palm Sunday, 2015

It's different benched, anonymous in the pew.
Herded by ushers (a scourge in bright red ties)
and draped in Sunday-best civility,
you mumble "Crucify" with lowered eyes.
Ecce! Deniability.
No one can pin this bloody death on you.

But when the text is written to be sung
by tenor, bass, and your own mezzo voice
and *Crucify him* is yours, a long melisma strung
across a shiver of neums, a poise
in arabesque, a steel point that will race
to ring the bonebound hollows of your face,
through all the shimmering pillar of air that's you

there is no way, no way, no bloody way
to know not what you do.

As Little Children

When the toddler-in-arms behind me
shouts "Cake!" at the elevation,
that's sliced it: my concentration
is toast, Abba. And all
I'm seeing now is *party.*
Jingling above the prayers,
an ice cream peddler's bell.
Communion as musical chairs.
Candles as candles. Songs.
Even a birthday crown:
Saint Margaret, Princess of Hungary,
her glazed smile sunbeaming down.
Not quite the party I wanted,
but it serves. I've come to feel
how all my feasts are haunted—
some holy, wounded memory
hanging above the meal.

Prayer Concerning the New, More "Accurate" Translation of Certain Prayers

O Lord of the inverted verb,
You Who alone *vouchsafe* and *deign,*
Whom simpler diction might perturb,
To Whom we may not make things plain,
Forgive us now this Job-like rant:
These prayers translated plumb-and-squarely
Pinch and constrict us (though we grant
They broaden our vocabulary).
Hear us still if we mutter dully
With uninflected tongues and knees,
Shunning (see Matthew 6) the poly-
Syllables of the Pharisees.
This we entreat, implore, beseech
Whose miseries are too deep for speech.

Pelicans at Nags Head

After a wedding at Manteo

Bumbling, ungainly, sag-chinned, laughable:
on land, the pelicans concede their natures.
Hugging the sand, one tries to hide his features,
long neck scrunched into shoulders, abashed bill
well down.

     Airborne, they're different: choreographed.
Baroque *danseurs*, their slow-beat wing pavane
impends above the waves. Suddenly, one
will fold and plummet, as though pure verve laughed
at want.

     All week, against the bottle-green
of low tide after late-spring storms that smashed
our summer piers to gray debris, I've seen
my earthbound family, like the birds I watched,
waiting for such a lifting to arrive:

women gleaming, men in dark formation
slow-poised toward this altar, while Bach's air
lofts us beyond self-consciousness and fear.
Gathered to rise, we brave by calm procession
this thrilled hunger, this stunning, headlong dive.

Syringa vulgaris "Victor Lemoine"

Victor Lemoine, hybridizer, 1823–1911

You always thought they were pure gift, the lilacs.

No work involved. Plain tendencies of nature,
those arcing stems, lavender panicles
of double flowers, draping the potholed alleys
still winter-littered in May, yet washed with fragrance
spring after spring, the thirty years you've lived here.
So free that the shoots invade the lawn unlooked-for.
Some years, the children help themselves to armfuls.

My dear, how like you. Effort is beyond you,
who slumped in boredom while your eighth-grade teacher
spun out the lacework rhyming of those patterns
conjured by Mendel from his plots of peas.

Have you once thought of the steady generations,
the grand *famille Lemoine,* the years of waiting?
Of Victor, blue-smocked, rapt in concentration
there in the greenhouse, gloved, his tiny brushes
tickling stamens, dusting gold to pistils?
Of hothouses in ranks, green as absinthe?

You who twiddle and fidget in line for coffee,
can you conceive whole countrysides in labor
at birthing these particular notes of purple?
Van Gogh-deep skies, Monet at Giverny?
Whole hills, whole valleys full of lavender
laid in with linen to stanch the coming bloodbath?

These are beyond you. Cost and pain, beyond you.
Take up your pruners; fill a generous vase
with the bruised color of that human tension.
Its perfume breathes the century away.

A Choral Ode

Oof. It's five-fifteen
and in the half-lit proto-dawn
cacophony kicks in: *Tu-whit! Cheerio!*
Every cliché for bliss your groggy ear has ever heard
fluting from old cartoons

pipes up. Pick out a bird
(one ear's awake now): robin; vireo;
house wren, in reticent gray-fawn,
chirruping at the screen;

blue jay in mid-scream;
cardinals' downward-arcing cries.
Keep listening: has an ache like a bad tooth
seeped through the sound, an undernote of fluttered
desperation?
(Crack of a shattered eggshell.

Whoosh of high migration.)
And haven't birding friends hinted the truth?
That all this twittering implies
some less-than-peaceful theme?

Well, let 'em chirr and cheep
like Looney Tunes. To heck with facts:
This jangling's more genteel than people's wars,
with costume party reveille in summertime backyards
and air corps kitted out

like crazy-quilt Swiss Guards.
In diplomatic wisdom, one ignores
such ruffled-feather noise. Relax.
Lie back again, and sleep.

Ardors

What makes the engine go?
Desire, desire, desire
　　　　—Stanley Kunitz

As if the sin of Adam took its toll
on trees, the maples stricken with the fall
burn in their sins. Red passion and proud gold,

their vanities float down like scraps of flame.
Lives ago, we burned them—garden stubble
and leaves—the yard's year gone in a smoky plume

curling to heaven. Now the tumulus
of compost seethes in its center, simmers, mulls.
We rake the piles. The crickets' wings rehearse

desire, desire, slowing as daylight's slant
unwarms the world. We feel it too, the chill,
the ache displacing older, wilder want:

Leaf into loam, red giant to black hole,
lust into languor, everything that burns
burns out: the dust, the gas, the acrid smell,

the end of the matter. All our burning's doomed,
even these fires where maple trees are found
still ardent after years, still unconsumed.

October

I fail at them, those scenes
where beauty is married to fear.
I have failed before with this one.
How can I make it clear

when the moment itself was a blur?
My son and I, that night,
stepped through the warm, wet air
that had magicked every light

to a wide, all-hallowing halo.
He said—I think he was ten,
still with his clear soprano—
It's lovely out here.

                              And then
the edge of every nimbus,
pale gold through a fog scrim,
shivered, knowing that beauty soon
would be bullied out of him.

Saccharomyces cerevisiae, or
A Little Levity about Leaven

Because, in its stubby brown-glass jar
        or its battered, three-personed foil packet,
        it gets entombed in the chaos of cartons
        appearing at last, as though resurrected,

Because the lump in which it lies hidden
        is formless and potent as creation's clay,

Because I sink my hands in its history
        and come up with *levamen*—
        "solace" or "consolation,"

Because it's consoling to smack it down—
        pummel it, grinning like a Halloween demon—
        and find I never defeat it,

Because its down-and-up-again persistence
        is like a congregation's kneeling and rising
        (*Levate,* in the Latin of old rubrics),

Because, at some point in the fifty years
        since I learned to file its fungal names
        among the tangled roots of the *Plantae*,
        they bloomed, those names, as a kingdom of their own,

And because this makes me smile, recalling
        that leaven's Your own little joke about the Kingdom,

Be praised, O Lord, for this bit of mystery,
        which lifts, which lightens.

To the Unknown God

*Upon the installation of the house-
hold's optical network terminal*

Welcome, newest of idols
sitting zazen, blinking
asynchronous emerald eyes,
and humming a megabyte mantra

from a shelf close to the fuse box,
that gray-clad holy of holies
meditating its Ohm.

You will be fickle; we know this.
All our nether-world watchers
have failed us time and again.

The hulking bull-god Boiler
has leaked at a gasket, spewing
lustral waters on the cat box.

The water heater, slim, white,
pure as a temple column,
went marble-cold to the landfill.

We kept our part of the covenant.
They left us wholly comfortless
in a two-faced January.

And here we are, like ancients
shaky in the old religion,
yet hauling new deities in

to a pantheon of deadbeats,
while we glance over our shoulders
at the town gates. Oh, they rattle!

But we shall admit your priests
for regular ministrations
and make our votive offerings
with every turn of the moon.

Late Intrusion

Tossing. Two a.m.
Strung out on latte, blue light,
and a world unhinged,

I'm pierced by the stare
of this knife-edged winter moon
slant, through bedroom blinds.

Shaking my brain loose,
I invoke Li Bai, although
our bed is not quite

his moon-filled river.
Still, on our undulant sheets
and bodies' currents

strips of moon ripple.
Light so hard, so bright the blinds
lay down white slices—

Ah, but that's Larkin
mooning for lost youth, and not
old Li Bai, drowning

in the moon's embrace.
No, I'm cold sober, barred from
both those lost lushes:

Virtuous Sidney,
courtier, soldier, tracker
of the moon's sad steps,

teach me to greet her
with your own graceful longing
(but a different plea,

since I lie beside
the very love you groaned for,
poor unsleeping soul).

Speak, Memory. Or Not.

This cute cafe, these college kids at a table,
this brunch I'm sharing with my children's crowd.
I tick off novelties amid the babble—
tattoos and piercings, earphones up too loud—

but jeans are changeless, and the young men's hair
is long, as achingly long as it was back then.
(I clamp my mouth shut tightly. Fair is fair;
this is their time; these are my daughter's men.)

And talk rehashes topics I'd have heard,
subject for subject, several decades gone:
the war, the sexes (almost word for word),
politics, jobs, the same mad rattling on—

I will decline to comment. They don't need
my sage advice, nor do they need to know
this priceless and expensive life they lead
was lived already. Or how long ago.

To the Anti-Librarian

Small vandal, parked on your padded bum
on a cheerful rug in the Children's Section
    next to a bottom shelf,
yanking the volumes one by one
till they strew the aisle in every direction,
    loudly pleased with yourself
at the way your brightly patterned havoc
    obstructs the traffic,

keep to your task. Disrupting order
is evolution's eternal purpose.
    Surely it's been *your* goal
from the hour two gametes burst their border
and two tame selves went wild as a circus.
    Systems that once felt whole
eyeballed each other, laughed, and gambled,
    and lives got scrambled.

Do your worst, then, with giggles, rage,
and all the smackdown-loud rebellion
    grown-ups are now too tired for.
These sleepless two, in a golden age,
were a black-clad goth and a hard-rock hellion.
    Change is the charge we're wired for.
Small changer, blessings. Though elders frown,
    pull the world down.

Collaborative Translation

Alas, they have had words.
No phrase in the target language
exhales the same fragrance—
clove and crankcase oil—
as that in the original,
the closest equivalent pressing
with the heft of petals and pine shavings
on his ear, while to hers
it tastes of light and stone dust.
Each night the poem mocks them.

They Consult the Home Repair Manual

These are new terms.
Pieces that framed
Their sliver of world
Had gone unnamed—
Unthought of, really—
Before today.
(Muntin? Mullion?)
Then views gave way
And openings stuck,
Iron-weighted.
(Sash cord. Stool piece.)
Perhaps it was fated
To fall out thus:
With him in his socks,
Holding the breakage
While she mocks
The shuttered outlook
Both will pay for,
Words they lived by
Splintered away for
Years now. Decades.
(Briefcase. Folder.)
Signals clenched
Between ear and shoulder
(Handset, earpiece)
Stammer, emphatic
While thoughts they stood for

Drift to static,
Disconnecting
Phones and memes.
A semiotics
Cracks at the seams.

What They Told Me

It was brief, and a freak storm, though the sleet stung.
It was dripped on a silk drape with a soft sheen.
It was heels on a hard floor, and the sound rang.
It was tiny, a white grub, but it wormed in.

It was light, and a clear dawn, yet it froze hard.
It was stuck in an orb web with a dead fly.
It was bitter and sweet, crumbed like a strange bread.
It was stark as a tack's point in a live eye.

It was chanted by rote, droned like an old rite.
It was silver with gold trim but a steel clasp.
It was blunt as the blind fist of a brute fate.
It was singing the wrong tune, and the turn passed.

Hoarder

The mess it makes, dear God: mountains of crap
spewed on the lawn, obscenely disarrayed.
Whatever sort of order her mind made
of this—crateloads of paper, whole and scrap;
torn couches (drunkenly tipped, upholstery damp
in the spring drizzle); bolts of stained brocade—
is violated. Dumped like a corpse. The date
came, and the truck, and the dumpster, dollies, and ramp
of the cleanout crew. Her cut-rate obit, bare,
boxed in the local paper's tidy square,
painted a straight-edged life. It wasn't true.
And now what's spilling from the garbage bins
lays bare before the world our local sins:
She was a hoarder, and we never knew.

We never knew. We knew she got her mail,
and scuffed outdoors in slippers for the flyers
left on the walk, mincing, as though by braille.
We didn't like to snoop. Should *we* be pryers
into her fenced-off life? It was enough
to see that someone shoveled, someone mowed.
And in subzero weather, the white puff
of a working furnace was a sort of code
for *All-is-well-enough-leave-it-alone.*
The porch light still fell feebly in gold pools
onto the graying snow. We had our own
troubles: rezoning, trash collection, schools,
taxes that burgeoned, dandelions that bloomed.
Dailiness ate us up. We were consumed.

We were consumed? I keep on saying *we*.
Let's talk about my own consuming passions,
the matter I've amassed for sixty years,
I and my spouse. At least our progeny
have flown, trailing their jettisoned possessions,
yet overnight we crammed space that was theirs
with things: books that seemed vital in the moment;
music, its living soul encased in vinyl.
What happened to the frugal hippie bride
I thought I was? What if it had to go—
everything, by some deadline, settled, final?
Fervent recycling wouldn't stem the tide.
The angel might as well begin recording
the worst: I *am* a hoarder. This is hoarding.

Yeah, hoarding. But the *stuff* is not the worst.
The worst is what the body can't unload.
Memory's bad enough when it's the goad
you kick against to trash the things it cursed.
(The dinnerware that graced the very worst
meals of your younger life, china by Spode,
glass by Lalique?) But memory can explode
in pain unpurchased, pain you were coerced
into the bearing of. (The fractured marriage
that fouled your mother's years down to her death,
its sadness handed down.) *Traditio*,
that quake you didn't feel, still leaves its wreckage.
Yours now, it keeps its pressure on your breath.
Worse than the stuff you own is the stuff you know.

The family stuff I know, down in my bones.
The world's junk hangs around in the tainted air,

a vague particulate matter, but it's there.
Sometimes my reading stirs it, and it moans
like Dickens's floating Christmas spirits. Groans
rise from the past, translated by the best
in prose and verse, and humankind's unrest
comes wailing from the ancient combat zones.
Or the rich years postwar, whose lead exhaust
coughs on. Or the misogynistic blather
of every body-loathing Latin Father.
Or the long foghorn of the Holocaust—
It deepens, Larkin says, like a coastal shelf,
this mess. Beyond Marie Kondo herself,

this mess, and inescapable in life.
To get past stuff, it seems you have to die.
The real life-changing magic, Dante says,
comes when you take the step beyond belief
and into matter-less eternity
where the unblinding Brightness purifies.
How long a flensing does it take a soul
twisted by decades clenched around its hoard
(would Dante classify that pain as Greed?)
to shake its brittle shell off and uncoil?
Pain cleanses—that's the theory—and you're spared.
Look up; the Light is everything you need.
This is the theory. And I'll hope for this
for my poor neighbor, may she rest in peace—

In peace? And then the last line of the Creed—
the resurrection of the body and
life everlasting—snaps me back. I need
to get things clearer. Where we finally stand
is in our bodies? Bodies made of *stuff*?
It's difficult to hear this as good news:
The fear that guts the concept of *enough,*
the gore that everlastingly ensues,
the epics of it, branded on the brain—
How bodies slough the awful heft of hoarding
is something theologians don't explain
but promise. And for now we're stuck here, Lord:
these bodies, and this stuff, and this distress.
The mess, dear God. Forgive us for the mess.

A Vision of St. Polycarp, Martyr, as Bartender

Flaming Blue Jesus? No, a different cocktail—
    less sacrilegious
but more flamboyant in its execution.
    The liquor mixed
and lit, the barman poured it from one raised tankard
    into another
he held above the glass-topped bar like a juggler,
    letting fall
through the half-dark a tongue of azure fire.
    A pleasant magic,

till the flame groped his arm. Then twenty people
    sucked in one gasp,
yet in a miracle of calm and deftness
    he set it down,
the drink, burning and blue, and with a shake
    was merely flesh

again. Why did I think then of that martyr
    whom the flames shrank from
when he stood ready to be burned for Jesus,
    and how, in faithless
places, there could be flaming chalices
    and fires that swayed
away from a body, billowing like sails?

    What could we say then?
We drank and wandered back into a street
    polished with drizzle,
still looking for some fire to take us on.

Buying a Plot in Plague Time

after Larkin

Shouldn't the moment be more—well, dramatic?
Shouldn't it toll like Donne's dead-bell? But no.
Mere paper-rustling. It's a burst of static
That stutters off to silence, while late snow
Alights outside and melts forgettably,
A numb reminder. Nothing I can see
In the small print addresses dread, or God,
Or love. Somber reflection? Not a bit.
Forms in quadruplicate:
White over yellow, pink, and goldenrod,

For a dead end. No hymns, no holiness—
No funeral; every gathering spreads the plague.
Perfunctory forms depress me, and they press
Me now, because I've left so much so vague.
When until now has dying loomed so real
I shrank from my dead flesh? Or when did I feel
This keen to leave less horror for my son
And daughter? Save them shock-and-awe about
Choices, when mine run out?
I mutter grimly, *I will get this done.*

And still I sit here, playing my numbers game,
Tossing my rhyme-pairs into the winds of fear.
Back to the labor. Back to the minor shame
Of shuffling off my life (check there, sign here).
Earth gets my ashes—grudgingly, on terms

That reek of real estate and legal firms.
Transfer-on-death arrangements and new will
Spew gray phrases: drone and drone and drone.
Like worrying a bone,
This work to stifle terrors I can't kill.

So work—bending the spirit to the letter,
Bowing the head at how the flesh unweaves—
Goes down like a stiff drink; the ache's no better
Yet, for the iron aftertaste it leaves.
Here, plague: take this dull prose; spare those I love.
I sign at all the Xs (and to prove
My resoluteness, press hard on the pen),
Scribble the check and seal the envelope.
Clinging weakly to hope,
I thumb the stamp on. No one says Amen.

Epinikion on Marshall Avenue

Up and down this alley of student rentals,
ritual takes hold of a waning weekend:
late October, Indian summer, ash trees
    showering leaf-gold

on backyardlets churning with youthful bodies,
muscled, sweat-slick, bawdy, lit up with victory,
drunk and singing, roaring the last hurrahs of
    Homecoming game day.

Noise, grill smoke, and memory hold the neighbors
spellbound at it all, at the pure unknowing
lifted up in these chesty pop-punk odes and
    beery libations—

This will pass. We've watched it for thirty autumns,
thirty springs. School ends, and the heroes scatter,
U-Hauled off as tribute to golden bull-gods.
    Will they survive it?

May this breeze and the scent of meat on firepits
rise to heaven, into the flames of sunset.
May that ancient fragrance appease some godhead.
    Kudos, O victors.

The Last Night at Porky's

Lords of the custom cars, where will they cruise
with Porky's gone? What drive-in's neon haze
will fold them in the glow of ancient days?
Where will they flaunt the metalflake chartreuse,
the pink/magenta, two-toned as a bruise,
or stroke a curve, or fondle a streamlined grace?
Beyond the final love-feast in this place,
where will lowriders slide through velvet-blues
of summer dusk, with the Big Bopper blaring?
Bare-domed, gray-ducktailed, who will love them back
to full communion with the holy names—
Packard, Studebaker, Pontiac,
de Soto? Shutters lower. Now they are staring
at sunset, candy-mauve, painted with flames.

Fr. Kleinsorge, *Hibakusha,* Celebrates Mass for August 6, the Feast of the Transfiguration

Because he lived till 1977,

> *his hair as white as wool*

surviving the effects both of the bomb

> *his throne flames of fire*

and of the great liturgical reform,

> *with wheels of burning fire*

he would have heard, on the remembered day

> *a stream of fire, surging*

each year in his last seven, the new readings

> *clouds and darkness about him*

from Daniel and the 97th Psalm

> *the mountains melting like wax.*

Apophatic

O absent Mind, blank where I fire this prayer,
tongue-tangled Word my neurons flash into flesh
because they must, might you be this: a brash-
ness of Terrible Two whose wild career
of sheer will muddles all my mother-care?
whose not-a-care heaves flood and avalanche?
lets blocky Towers tippy-topple and crash?
giggles delight while crackhead comets steer
headlong at little worlds? Might you be this:
all pink-cheeked lovable but not yet master
at seeing your lovely patterns as disaster?
so rapt up in unwinding fiddle-ferns
you think death changes nothing?
                                        No. This is
all error. But it helps me come to terms.

Monuments

Pioneers and Soldiers Cemetery, Minneapolis

They look us in the face. Their brokenness
is scarred where bits are grafted back with mortar,
their attitude off-kilter where the world's
upheavals knock them sideways. Their stone speech
comes garbled through the acid bite of rains
sour with the hundred-fifty-year-long progress
that vaunts down Lake Street in the August glare
outside the wall's wrought-iron rectitude.

Each stands, a presence. Bevels, obelisks,
round-shouldered roundtops, green cast-metal crosses,
three regimented rows of Civil War
martyrs (a name, a date, the one word "soldier"),
a few actual statues. Where the words
are legible, here German and there Polish
keep their detente, the long truce undisturbed
by a versified Last Trumpet. So the thought
of variousness feels apt, an old-shoe comfort
fit for the neighborhood as it now stands,
its business signs relaxing into Spanglish.
And we stand, roughly vertical, if damaged.
Tolerant of our shorts and broad-brimmed hats,
the stones pose coolly while we snap our selfies.

My dead lie down a thousand miles away,
scattered across three states, in cemeteries
run with a view to simplifying upkeep.
Their rules enforce a flat equality:
no standing stones to look us in the eye,
only the flush bronze markers, silhouetteless,
staring upward at God without a thought,
unfindable without a shamefaced visit
to some Dickensian ministry of death.
The snows of every winter white them out,
and with the summers, over all this absence
the great blade of the mower passes, sighing.

An Atomic Theory

Soul of Giordano Bruno,
you whose tongue and lips they stilled by nailing
(their opening act-of-faith)
surely the Lord of stubborn holdout sufferers
cradles you, martyr,

in that life you had no faith in.
Surely then I may plead for your intercession
against the useless urge
to rummage around in the space between the electrons
for the slippery Mystery

or to rattle my cerebellum
totting up the allotment of my atoms,
since I believe my God
will find some way to parcel my elements out
to the risen bodies

they've spent millennia making—
Shintoists, Mayans, Athabaskans, Frenchmen,
the odd Neanderthal.
I like to imagine that your heavenly joys
include this knowledge:

that the radio telescope
at Arecibo is sifting the universe
for the plural worlds you preached,
and that this vision of grace was granted you
just at the instant

when the soul you kept denying
slipped free, before the charred dust of your bones
could float on the humanist air
of Florence, past the fires of the Inquisition,
to its next recycling.

Alumni Magazine

New-evolved from gloss to matte,
crisp, flat-spined, and perfect-bound,
freshly issued twice a year,

calm in coffee-table state
here it lies. Open and watch
all life's losses disappear.

Undergrads in faultless poise
wear their scientific findings
garlanded with liberal arts.

(Out of view, the yet-to-be:
work, and all its weary windings,
blasted hopes and trampled hearts.)

Cynical, you say? Yes, well.
Turn the pages. In "Class Notes"
only sparkling news is spoken:

Himalayan climbing trip.
Book deal. (No one wants to read
Bankrupt. Homeless. Spirit-broken.)

And the dead? No list appears.
Failure too despised to name.
Once, I used to note them there—

cordoned off, as though unclean,
on a sable-bordered page—
back before I learned to care.

Still, here's Class of '56.
God forbid you photograph them
wheelchaired, addled, knuckle-gnarled.

Vale. Close the magazine.
Perfect face on flawless cover.
Best of luck, O brave new world.

Reading the Early Letters

i.m. Anthony Hecht

Why should it shock me that his younger self
spouts wordplay like a great baroque *jet d'eau,*
German abbreviations, French *bons mots,*
lettered allusions up and down the shelf
of the Bard's dramas? *And* the KJV?
Even in wartime, juggling bric-a-brac!
A bright disguise, put on for family?
A carapace his later poems would crack?

False questions. My small shudder at the heart
drums from the memory of those pinched and bland
and few scribbles I sent from school back then
to parents shy of words and starved of art.
All parties artless, failing to understand
what mattered—

        Fifty years, and I wince again.

Praying Sleepless

after Hudgins and Wilbur

O Lord, that last, late-evening cappuccino—
beautiful fuel of poets' conversations,
inspirer of wild readings and sweeping gestures,
intense, froth-headed, somewhat over-the-top—
that was poor judgment. Here I am again,
bug-eyed at midnight. Brain a wheeling hamster.
Groping the darkness for some ropey ladder
down to oblivion. Hauling You along.

You must know, Lord, You're awkward company.
Like that great-aunt, chintz-clad and over-scented,
who pursed her lips around the family secrets
and mumbled her long love in a gravelly accent
that baffled a small child. And I'm still baffled,
starting out with You. The formal approach?
The etiquette says, Start with adoration,

and right away I'm lost. What does adoring
feel like? Like fingers itching for a cell phone?
Eyes gorging big-screen candy, or gowns on the runway,
or the hyped whoever hurtling down a field?
Like awe, in the face of massiveness beyond me—
the Large Hadron Collider, the Horsehead Nebula,
the federal budget? Surely not. Start over.

I know; I'd do this better on my knees.
My body would instruct my gunning brain

in depth, concerning its wet-noodle weakness.
Forgive me, Lord. Kneeling would put off sleep
further. The bed's warm. Thank You for that,
and for the notion to take things out of order
and do thanksgiving first: For the loved body
next to me, and the wheezing of his CPAP,
and the little Martian-green light of the monitor
that stands as guardian angel over his heart,

though I haven't prayed in years to a guardian angel.
Lately they seem to be falling down on the job,
always shouted down by the sound of money,
or drugs, or fear of other people. Lord,
what happened to my childhood certainties?
Was it just recitation, when I knelt
on a little prie-dieu, in a grade-school hallway,
before the Infant of Prague, robed like an emperor
in satins matched to the liturgical season?

Or when I stood to intone the *Memorare*
crowned with silk flowers, in a blue lace semiformal
in church, before the May-procession crowd?
How do I deal with those period-piece locutions
stuffed with strained imagery and inverted grammar?
"To thee do we cry, poor banished children of Eve."
"Despise not my petitions." Even in private
the words sound wrenched, like a bad beginner's poem.

Where does that leave me, Lord, trying to pray?
Yes, there's the Gospel-certified *Our Father*—
but here be dragons, if you knew my father....

so praying crumbles away to the endless question,
Who are You, Lord? What do you want of me?
I hope You hear me, mumbling inside my skull.
You who are somewhere past the edge of spacetime,
somewhere within the null of the neutrino,
lure me off the cliff of my comprehension
the way Road Runner lures Wile E. Coyote,
so that I hang, know I am lost, and fall

and fall, into the surf of repetition,
hail Mary, holy Mary, hidden behind
the wave machine of mantra, aiming at You
but slantwise, down the curl. Just the one prayer,
beadless, uncounted. Now that I have seen
the hour of our death, the hours of four grim deaths,
the ashen hours and days of an almost-death—
I fumble there. I start again, *hail Mary,*
trusting the earth's divine maternal forces
to draw the weighted dark over my head.

Sacred Art & Architectural Salvage, Inc.

In the aftermath of the abuse investigations

Blessed is this warehouse: plaster-crumbed
    limbo of the souls of the gutted churches.

Blessed this gaggle of fonts, their marble bowls
    waterless as the deserts in Isaiah.

Blessed these tabernacles, gaping, empty,
    next to the painted rows of dry-eyed statues.

Blessed the drapery of stiff blue veils
    and pale curls of the manifold Madonna,
    whole rosaries of her, rote as grade-school prayer.

Blessed the satin robes in every color,
    trimmed in white lacework (frayed at hem or wrist)
    on ranks and files of the Infant-Jesus-of-Prague,

Round-cheeked and rosebud-lipped, as though no evil
    could ever soil a childish innocence.

Blessed this emptying, its dust and crumble
    the sackcloth of our humbling.

Blessed is salvage, waiting for salvation.

Funeral Road Trip

i.m. Timothy Murphy

The whole four hours to Fargo,
our engine bucked and stuttered
in bucketing rain, and we wondered
if a poet's intercession
would help a struggling car go,
when heaven itself remembered
the flash of his drunken passion

and yet we thought it answered:
three booms, distantly muttered—
the poet's clipped concision
but huge now, long now, *largo*.

Physical Therapy Gym,
Neuroscience Center

God? you're good at taking me as I am? Then
take me this way: craven, pusillanimous,
chickenshit. Teeth gritted, fists tight against the
    wrack of the body.

Wrench me back from whipping around to stare when
someone keens *I can't do it any longer,*
take me home, I want to go home. From hearing
    sobbing and chest-heave

gasps. Don't let me see. Let me see instead how
every other head in this hall of mirrors
sets itself like marble, tilting to face its
    torturer, smiling.

Votive Offering

"By donating your hair you can help a cancer patient to be healed."

A sacrifice, I thought: donate my hair.
To placate her dark gods, a plait of my hair.

A way of stretching toward her over miles—
toward retching, scars, steel plate beneath dry hair.

The slow growth. The weeks of time spent hanging,
flyaway, split. The strung-out state of my hair.

Long distances of talk. We curl around
the knotty problem. I can't yet braid my hair.

A year, while strands of cirrus slough from the sky.
Then everything cut short. Too late, my hair—

How thin, how worthless it looks, in its elastic
in the limp plastic bag where I laid my hair.

The gods of healing never learned my name.
Pointless to write it here. I hate my hair.

A Dream of Rooms

It goes like this. The house, he knows, is theirs.
Doors open into rooms he's never seen.
Light leans across the perfect hardwood floors.
Completely bare. Walls freshly painted, clean.

He enters. These are rooms he's never seen
or else their own rooms, stripped of pointless things.
The floors are bare. The walls are white now, clean.
Their early indiscretions in deep pinks

and greens have been absolved. The pointless things
that screwed themselves into his memory,
the pain of poor decisions, greens and pinks—
Gone. All has been somehow borne away.

The plastered-over holes of memory
don't show. The rats that gnawed his thoughts are dead,
and the whole past is somehow borne away.
A space opens beside him. On the bed

someone is not. And then his mind goes dead,
empty of everything but sun on floors.
A space shudders beside him on the bed.
He wakes then in the house he knows was theirs.

Another night, another load of corpses,

jostled out of the reeds by college rowers,
according to the local crime reportage.
Sinking, pack-laden, into the Normandy riptide
deep in a grainy late-night documentary.
Blue-lipped, mottled, chill on a coroner's slab
in this week's twenty-third detective thriller
or mud-bloody in Bosworth-Fieldian chaos.
(Shakespeare's? history's? It hardly matters.)
Bullets, gurglings, screams, ominous music:
the screen supplies us everything but the odor.

Does this explain why I was unprepared?
when, after hours of sitting beside my mother—
alone, flown hurriedly in from far away—
hours of rosaries, psalms, calm classical radio,
with no response apart from her changeless breathing,
I ducked into the hospice kitchen, thinking,
Might it be safe to break for a bit? Wolf down
my leftovers of spinach-and-cheese croissant?
and she, with her usual undramatic methods,
met God while I was paying no attention?

Responsorial Psalm for the Beneficiary of My Mother's Will

℣ *O Lord, You are my inheritance*

> ℟ unearthed from murky records,
> set down at tables where too little was said
> by kinfolk who hedged their memories

℣ *Yea, I have in you a goodly heritage*

> ℟ in a will laid out like an Edwardian banquet,
> its places set by gloved hands,
> precision ready to shatter

℣ *in you who are my portion and cup,*

> ℟ my place at a feast set by death,
> a dinner announced by unnerving letters from courts
> full of strange demands, like the dreams of prophets

℣ *my cup of blessing*

> ℟ delivered in the fullness of time
> by UPS, in a corrugated carton
> whose breached sides leak bubble wrap
>
> and unpacked at last: gold-rimmed, daintily painted,
> bone-white shimmer of longing
> for an ease there was never enough of

℣ *O Lord, You uphold my lot*

℟ which I hoard now at the back of a cupboard
accreting a fuzz of dust and kitchen grease,
a richness, O Lord,
too breakable for the living.

The Window Shoppers

Strolling the malls, in the bauble-bright late fifties,
My schoolmates' parents could be nonchalant.
Not mine. Already earners in the thirties,
They'd known the rancid tang of actual want
And window-browsing made their faces glow.
The daylong sourness on their tongues and teeth
Melted, there in the mall at Seven Corners.
Hope ringed their heads like a cigarette-smoke wreath.
Yet any actual purchase somehow came
Salted with supper-table arguments.
Grinding their teeth on loveliness, they dreamed.
Waking, they gripped the bills and scrounged the cents.
So now they have brushed platinum, ruched satin,
Rose-wreathed extravagance. The sort of waste
Their frugal heads would frown on, I have chosen.
God of abundance, let their starved souls taste.

Word Frequency Head Trip

Like is the yoke of a simile's pair.
God is the question, the O in the air.
Now is not now is not now. But it was.
End is the problem, since everything does.

Acknowledgments

I owe thanks to the editors of the following journals, where many of these poems appeared, sometimes in slightly different versions or with different titles:

Alabama Literary Review, America, Angle, Anglican Theological Review, The Arkansas International, Berfrois, Blue Unicorn, Christianity and Literature, The Classical Outlook, Connotation Press, The Curator, Dappled Things, The Dark Horse (UK), Ecotone, Evangelization and Culture, First Things, Innisfree Poetry Journal, kaleidowhirl, Lavender Review, Lief, LIGHT, Literary Imagination, Literary Matters, Measure, Measure Review, Mezzo Cammin, Modern Age, The Other Journal, Poetry Salzburg Review, Presence, The Raintown Review, Rattle, Relief, The Rotary Dial, Saint Katherine Review, Sewanee Theological Review, The Somerville Times, SWWIM, Tilt-a-Whirl, Umbrella, Whistling Shade, and *The Windhover.*

Thanks are also due to David Robert Books, Pudding House Press, Scienter Press, and the University of Evansville Press, publishers of my books *Breath Control* and *Mid Evil* and my chapbooks *Gardening in a Time of War* and *Dissonance*, in which seven of these poems were included.

"Ardors" appeared in the anthology *Imago Dei: Poems from* Christianity and Literature (Abilene Christian University Press, 2012).

"Circadian Lament …" appeared in *Love Affairs at the Villa Nelle* (Kelsay Books, 2018).

"Prayer Concerning ..." appeared in *The Best American Poetry 2018* (Scribner's, 2018).

"Rereading the *Aeneid* ..." appeared in *Measure for Measure: An Anthology of Poetic Meters* (Random House, 2015).

"Speak, Memory. Or Not." appears on *The Hypertexts* and appeared in the Potcake Chapbook anthology *Families and Other Fiascos* (Sampson Low, 2019).

"The Last Night at Porky's" appeared in the chapbook *University Avenue Sonnets: A Crooked Crown* (Kraken Books, 2012).

"Word Frequency Head Trip" appears in Mary Meriam's online collection "Basic Me."

I am indebted to A. E. Stallings for the form of "Back Story," which is borrowed from her poem "Alice in the Looking Glass."

I also wish to thank editor James Matthew Wilson of Colosseum Books for his support of my work.

And as always, thanks are due to the poets, moderators, and administrators of Eratosphere.

About the Author

Maryann Corbett earned a doctorate in English from the University of Minnesota and expected to be teaching *Beowulf* and Chaucer and the history of the English language. Instead, she spent almost thirty-five years working for the Office of the Revisor of Statutes of the Minnesota Legislature, helping attorneys to write plain English. She is the author of three chapbooks and six full-length books of poetry. Her work has won or has been shortlisted for the Able Muse Book Prize, the Hollis Summers Prize, the Howard Nemerov Sonnet Award, the Morton Marr Prize, the Richard Wilbur Award, and the Willis Barnstone Translation Prize and has appeared in many journals on both sides of the Atlantic as well as an assortment of anthologies, including *The Best American Poetry 2018*. Her poems have been featured on Poetry Daily, Verse Daily, American Life in Poetry, the Writer's Almanac, and the Poetry Foundation website. She lives in Saint Paul, Minnesota.

Also by Maryann Corbett

Breath Control
Credo for the Checkout Line in Winter
Mid Evil (Richard Wilbur Award, 2014)
Street View
In Code